PEACH CREEK

MARK APEL

LUCK BURDEN PRESS

Copyright © 2024 by Mark Apel

All rights reserved.

No part of this book may be reproduced in any form or by any electronic or mechanical means, including information storage and retrieval systems, without written permission from the author, except for the use of brief quotations in a book review.

"Do You Remember That One Time?," "The Bug in the Magazine," "Porch Light," "June Bug," "The Dragonfly," "Beetle with a Broken Wing," "Cement Drawer," "Crawdad," "The Place of Dreams," "Geckos," "Plume," "Holy Wild Days," "Whatever Ponds Are Left," "Turner Falls," "Mating for Life," "Blue Jays," "Vulture," "Write What You Know," and "Your Light" were previously released in Mark Apel's book, *Holy Wild Days*, published by Outset Editions in April 2021.

Cover design by Bret Hawkins.

For Porter

When I heard the learn'd astronomer,
When the proofs, the figures, were ranged in columns before me,
When I was shown the charts and diagrams, to add, divide, and measure them,
When I sitting heard the astronomer where he lectured with
much applause in the lecture-room,
How soon unaccountable I became tired and sick,
Till rising and gliding out I wander'd off by myself,
In the mystical moist night-air, and from time to time,
Look'd up in perfect silence at the stars.

— WALT WHITMAN, *LEAVES OF GRASS*

CONTENTS

I. Insects & Arthropods	9
Porch Light	11
Do You Remember That One Time?	13
Mosquito Hawks	15
The Dragonfly	17
June Bug	19
My Spider, My Tenant	21
Beetle with a Broken Wing	25
Cement Drawer	27
Crawdad	29
The Place of Dreams	31
Mud Towers	33
The Bug in the Magazine	35
II. Mammals, Reptiles, & Amphibians	37
Bull Frog	39
Trust	41
Exhibit	43
Zebra	45
Geckos	47
Evening Bat	49
III. Birds	51
Blackbird	53
A Kettle of Kites	55
Plume	57
Crows	59
Whatever Ponds Are Left	61
Turner Falls	63
Mating for Life	65
Blue Jays	67
Vulture	69
Junco	71
Snow Jay	73
IV. Water, Trees, Houses, & Humanity	75
Underwear	77
Swimsuits	79

Weeds	81
Companion	83
Write What You Know	85
Maple Tree	87
Boot	89
The Station at Marietta	91
Heater	93
Your Light	95
About the Author	97
Also by Mark Apel	99

I. INSECTS & ARTHROPODS

PORCH LIGHT

I left the porch light on last night,
A sense of security,
Keeping the would-be burglars at bay,
Drawing the light-drunk June bugs in.
Supposedly, while we were sleeping,
Insectual debauchery ensued,
And as I let the dogs out this morning,
Drinking in the first moments
Of fresh morning sun,
I saw a hungover brownish beetle
Staggering off the patio
Back into blades of safe St. Augustine,
Leaving behind a few of his brothers,
Their knobby legs barely moving,
Still lying on their backs.

DO YOU REMEMBER THAT ONE TIME?

Do you remember that one time,
When the power went out,
And we knew we were going to die?
Our bodies scattered
Throughout the neighborhood,

By the hand of God,
Having seen our sins,
Knowing our thoughts,
He sent a low-pressure cell to South Texas?

And, if you remember,
At some point after midnight,
We must have fallen asleep,
And the storm blew through,

Nothing but a few downed trees,
Hail-damaged minivans,
And the creek rose,
And we weren't dead.

All that to say,
Do you remember that ball of fire ants
We saw floating near the bridge,

Bobbing in the brown waters?

I still remember it.
I had a dream about it last night, actually,
Linking legs in mouths,
Desperately banding together,

Floating down a nameless stream,
Being picked apart by silver shad,
Taking turns on the bottom,
Holding their breath.

It felt good to remember
When it flooded back home.
I bet no one else even thinks
About that stuff anymore.

MOSQUITO HAWKS

Mosquito Hawks are
Sleeping on the eastern wall
Near the humming vents.

THE DRAGONFLY

Might be the cousin of the butterfly,
With a darker story, like a
Monarch with a tattoo,
Grazing the overgrown grass
For whatever it is it eats.
Its tail, presumably
The most dangerous of stingers,
Is in fact simply a tail.

Wings change direction
Like the changing of radio stations,
A constant toggling between AM, FM,
Morning news, traffic reports, pop songs,
Conservative family conversation,
And a special on wildlife conservation.

He never stops, this dragonfly,
And as I walk from porch to mailbox to porch
I dare not look at return addresses
Much less the contents of envelopes,
Fixing my eyes on the Mystical Purple
Maneuvering through blades
Of dehydrated Bermuda and spurge weed.

Then as I enter the house, I begin my poetry.
I must not allow the essence
Of dragonfly to end.
I pen and I paper,
And I question my questions...
Am I the fly? Or is it you?
No, you are the blades of grass and me,
Maybe I am the butterfly's cousin?
Or maybe the dragonfly is exactly
The dragonfly, and you are you, and I,
Well I guess I have to be me.

But if I could choose, and I most assuredly will,
I would definitely be the cicada
Perched on the fence
That we haven't even discussed yet.

JUNE BUG

Is this the ideal life for a June bug?
Reaching towards the porch light
But landing in my hair.

MY SPIDER, MY TENANT

She didn't write me messages like Charlotte
In the corner of my home office
I did come to enjoy her, however,
Her black spindle frame,
Her constant presence,
Cool and aloof.

I imagined she enjoyed me too—
Her abdomen wagging, like a pup,
When my bale of hair rounded the corner
To sit at my cheap desk and chair,
To type out the morning words.

I was not afraid of venom,
I was not afraid of her TV screen eyes,
It was the web that got to me,
And the way it collected each day's dust

But still, I let her stay.

When I couldn't think of a word
I would look to her,
No hints in her web.
I watched as she moved

Her two front legs
Almost imperceptibly
To tuck in a stray strand.

I admired the delicacy
She gave to the trapping,
Killing, and devouring
Of her homely harvests.

But how my week turned somber!
The house musty from the rain,
Not able to find my notes
From the day before,
My melancholia turned manic,
And once I found them,
Laying quietly uncovered on my desk,
They amounted to nothing of substance.

I nervously tidied the desktop
To make up for the failure of the morning,
A drawer for the books,
A case for the pens,
An unmarked file folder,
For all the loose sheets.

I wiped the emptied surface with my hand,
The dry, pale powder,
Snapping my compulsions,
Into focus and fervor.

My eyes shot to her web—its grayness
Marring the cream
Of the crown molding.

I was dead set,
I was determined,
I would rid this room of her hoarding
Of airborne cells and lacewing shells.

I lifted my ladder,
I climbed to my corner,
My chest heaving out
My murderous intent!

Oh, but there she was—
My spider.
Her appendages defensively curved,
Like a wilted bloom,
Alone and lifeless,
Oscillating in the damp draft
Coming from the open window,
Caught in her own web.

BEETLE WITH A BROKEN WING

You pointed out a beetle,
One with a broken wing
Outside the home where your grandmother
Had a single bedroom.

I made a note in my phone that said,
"Beetle with broken wing"
And, as it scuttled along,
I pictured the end of the story,

A magical realism read,
Where after all of the sickness,
After all of the atrophy,
The last chapter features her,

Still wrapped in her blankets,
In her chair,
Warm air still spilling from the heater,
Gospel music still spilling from the speaker,

But she, no longer forgetful,
Or aging,
Or losing her wits,

Was just a beetle, smiling,
Remembering everything,
Hard-shelled and healthy,
Temporarily grounded,
With a broken wing.

CEMENT DRAWER

I have this recurring dream
I am on my childhood street
The rain has just stopped
And everyone is inside.

Next to the house number
Painted on the curb
Is a drawer handle
Camouflaged as cement.

I pull on it
And out slides an old drawer
Filled with centipedes
And skittish hermit crabs.

There are gold coins,
A broken wristwatch,
And a few other heirlooms
Hiding under crustacean limbs.

Now, when I go to visit
And I glance over
To where the drawer should be,
I am glad to find it undisturbed.

CRAWDAD

How that crawdad
Got out of the seafood restaurant
And onto the sidewalk
Is beyond me,
But we saw it there,
Pinchers raised
Sort of defensive
But also as if to say,
"Move along, this doesn't concern you."

THE PLACE OF DREAMS

There are different versions of it
For this girl I met once
It was a mansion
Wrapped in vines of snakes
I heard one guy call it a jon boat
Stuck out on unknown waters
This veritable venue of sleep
I mention mine
Casually over coffee
In case they know the place
Maybe saw it on their drowsy
Walks from the mansion
Or have spotted it from the lost lake
Though no one yet knows mine
A two story brick home
Solo on a cul-de-sac
With a kitchen full of spiders
And a living room made of pure cloud
Out front is a broken down
Chevy Cheyenne I sometimes wake up in
And up the hill is an old billboard
Facing an empty highway of lights
Where I have spray-painted

Across both sides
"Sleep Well"

MUD TOWERS

When it rained,
We danced under the lightning,
Swabbing the muddy depths of ditches
With sticks and nets
In hopes of drawing out the crawdads.

We would place them
On the banks of Peach Creek,
Pincers raised,
Mine, ranked for size,
"Hail, Mighty Claw!"
And yours, ranked for speed,
"Godspeed, Crusty!"

Our constant replacement into the ring,
As these prisoners of war
Sought each their own escape,
Limping back to their cloudy silt-homes,
Towers of mud—their kingdoms!

Were they, perhaps, royalty?
Plucked from their duties
By our supermarket nets?
Forced to fight a war

They had already won?

When the rain fell,
Perhaps, given their continued armistice,
And stretching their plentiful
Translucent limbs,
They, too, danced under the lightning.

THE BUG IN THE MAGAZINE

I did not write the poem you asked me to,
When you opened the magazine
In the book store
And there in the middle,
Adjacent to the binding brads,
Sat a small, translucent bug.

You sensed the beginnings of a story,
How this beetle saw an opportunity,
Her escape from some dire, buggish tragedy,
Nestled into the pages
Of exquisite North American interiors
And died on her way to Barnes and Noble.

You said,
"You should write a poem about this,"
And I think now that perhaps you,
The one who really saw her,
Should have told her story.

II. MAMMALS, REPTILES, & AMPHIBIANS

BULL FROG

The turgid bull frog,
Warming on the smooth asphalt,
Sleeps like a tadpole.

TRUST

Trust is a cat
Hidden in the room
Until he is off
On some feline journey
Then suddenly in your lap
Purring in sweet peace
Just to tell you
He must be going now.

EXHIBIT

Translucent geckos
In the cracks of our ceiling
Watching us sleep in.

ZEBRA

We taught you how to swim in the bath—
Baptizing you in bubbles,
Cupping our hands to receive pretend hot tea
From the pitcher we rinse your hair with.

Each night you got better,
A new style achieved,
The fish, of course, was first,
Then, naturally, the frog
I taught you the turtle,
Your mom, the jellyfish,
But tonight,
All on your own,
And much to our endless delight,
You swam like a zebra.

GECKOS

Over twenty Mediterranean house geckos
In a red Igloo cooler,
A temporary terrarium.
Translucent legs and tails
All grasping at slick plastic walls.
The neighbors loved the show,
As we demonstrated their ability
To scale our arms in seconds,
As we stirred the panicked pink potion
In our make shift caldron
"Eye of newt," I cried
With a squinted witch-eye.

But after the novelty wore off
And the neighbor kids went inside for dinner,
I felt guilty for catching
And trapping the lizards.
And when I poured them out on the porch,
Helping a few find their favorite perches
Along the wall,
I became sad.
Maybe it was fatigue, even old age,
Or that show-biz was not the life for them,

But the three at the bottom
Weren't moving anymore.

EVENING BAT

You are unmistakeable,
You drunken dove of dusk.
I wish to have your wings
And sober wit,
To join you in the moth chase,
And to share with you
A nightcap of nectar.

III. BIRDS

BLACKBIRD

Of all the black birds
You are the most frightening—
pointed beak and eyes.

A KETTLE OF KITES

A swarm of Mississippi Kites
Has taken up residence in the neighbor's tree,
A large Magnolia
With fragrant blooms sharing branches
With the blue-gray birds of prey.

They eat the local field mice off of the land
Left to be developed into homes at a later date.
Their screeches bounce off
Each of our four walls,
Talons gripping the power lines
That fuel our televisions
And washing machines.

What is it that they want?
Are they here for good?
Research reveals this swarm to be called
A "brood," or "roost," or "kettle."

"A kettle of Mississippi Kites
Has taken up residence in the neighbor's tree,"
Sounds much warmer.
Much more welcoming.

PLUME

Feathers blowing across a field
And I, a single gray one
Like the others,
Silent and similar
Moving away from our bird
Toward our futures in gutters,
Nests, and dream catchers
And, if lucky, as a pen—
A feather's highest postmortem calling.
Though currently, a host-less tuft
Mixed among dust and breezes.

But as the wind dies,
And we oscillate toward the earth,
Enters you, the blushing exotic
With a speckled white tip
Fading into rosy down,
A slender plume
Fresh off the wing,
Riding the slightest breeze,
Rolling and twisting,
Showing us your color,
Pushing this grey mob with you,
And giving us all,

Even if just for a moment,
The chance to dance with you,
Or at least, given your gusts,
The hope to land our tired quills
In the inkwell.

CROWS

Two crows protesting
The white on the tops of trees
And the slush in the streets.

WHATEVER PONDS
ARE LEFT

For a certain amount of money
You gave up ownership
Of this swath of land,
That I had no stake in
By any means,
Except whatever ownership comes
From simple viewership.

The goats went away first.
There were small signs of sale,
But when the cows were loaded up.
It felt final.

And today, as the Canada Geese flew in
I felt it, quite deeply.
Several times a year they are here,
As you know,
And this time their pond,
Near the road, was drained.

With their tired wings
Pressed tightly to their sides,
The pads of their triangle feet
Buried in inches of mud,

They drank out of the little pools
That remained in tractor ruts.

Next year
They will return to concrete,
To homes and cars,
Like parents showing their kids
Where they used to live.

The remnants of their pond
Will be bricked and partitioned.
Thankfully, a small park will be nearby
Where human children will gather,
Pointing and shouting
At the downy, baby birds.

Bread will be thrown,
And the geese will leave
For whatever ponds are left.

TURNER FALLS

The park was empty,
The geese cautiously eating
Something off of the lawn,
The sounds of falling water,
And the sights of Turkey Vultures,
Leaning into smaller
And smaller circles,
Reminding me to keep moving,
To look alive.
And on the rusty stairwell
Leading down to the cave
Which over looks the falls,
Was a weathered sticker
Perfectly placed to catch my eye
On my way back from a hike,
Reminding me that a metal band,
Whose sun-bleached name
Looking something like *MurderDeath*,
Was playing a nearby show
On the 13th of some month in 2013.

I hoped deep in my heart,
As I caught my breath
At the top of the Arbuckle Mountains,

For the sake of music,
For the sake of the listeners,
And especially for the members
Of *MurderDeath*,
That their concert was on a Friday.

MATING FOR LIFE

I've heard many times,
"Swans are one of the only other animals
That mate for life,"
As if people are the poster children
Of sticking it out.
A simple internet search
Proves them wrong with
Barn owls, beavers, bald eagles,
And termites.
So not only are they wrong,
But they are up there with the termites.
And couldn't we use a bit more research?
Like, do the beavers,
After raising a few kittens,
And getting them into some
Nice dams of their own,
End up parting ways?
Do some bald eagles,
After slowly growing apart,
Decide they no longer love each other?
What about the conscious uncoupling
Of the barn owls?

Oh my sweet and precious termite,

Let us beat the odds,
With the weight
Of the soggy wood on our backs,
Let us give the microscopes
The story they need,
So that somewhere,
Some couple,
Will read our article,
In some glossy science magazine,
And say,
If the termites can do it...

BLUE JAYS

I love how big Blue Jays are,
And it's not even that they're that big,
More like I had forgotten
The exactness of their size,
As if I had gotten used to
The finch and the falcon
Both finding respite near the apartment,
But when the Jay flies in,
Twiddling its tail feathers a bit,
Checking the wind,
I am shocked at his median girth.
Sure, his blueness is a pleasure to see too,
But, seriously, have you considered its size?

VULTURE

Oh how I've grown to love you
You black-billed terror
Gliding over houses
Cleaning our streets
In my hunt for hawks
All I see is you
Bald faced, ugly, you.
Posting up for the night
On the street lamp
Dreaming your haunted
Carrion-dreams

I have grown to love you
In the morning
As you hop on spindled legs
Out of way of sedans
And delivery trucks
As you sniff out the day's
Roadside offerings

So I say eat the spoiling rabbit
Right in front of the kids
Returning home from school, by all means

For I have grown to love you
And you can do no wrong.

JUNCO

There is a Dark-eyed Junco
Skipping branches in the juniper—
With its acidic, sweet berry scent
And the river sauntering underneath.

There is a circle of rocks,
Bits of lava,
At some point having trickled
Down the mountain,

Just north of the falls and rapids,
Forming an exquisite eddy,
And in it, drinking and cleaning
Its fierce talons and petite beak,
Is another Dark-eyed Junco.

I long to be this bird,
Not the Steller's Jay in the spruce,
Nor the Scrub Jay below the Oregon grape,
But this Junco in this eddy,

To let loose my human compulsions
To embrace the life of a wild bird,
To disassociate with the way

Of domesticated ruin,
To let the snowmelt drip down my beak
To find its way between my feathers,
And to inherit the anxieties,
Fears, shame, and regrets
Of the Dark-eyed Junco.

SNOW JAY

Was that a Blue Jay
Spinning in the branches
While the snow came down?

IV. WATER, TREES, HOUSES, & HUMANITY

UNDERWEAR

Yesterday I swam
In only my underwear
In Aunt Jan's pool.

SWIMSUITS

Swimsuits hang and dry
On the curtain rod at home
Until December.

WEEDS

It's interesting to me
That we don't fertilize the weeds.
Yet they grow faster than the Augustine,
Seeds like kites,
The handle in my neighbors garden,
The string across our fence,
The tail and main sail nestling in my sod.

I watched the seed germinate
And grow leaves with teeth,
A monster birthed
Under the most promising of circumstances.

How shocked I was to see my hydrangeas,
Purple and blue, wither within weeks.
How strange it seemed,
When I watched insects land and die,
And witnessed the weed eating my Shih Tzu,
Then taking over my patio furniture.

How quickly I grabbed my bag
And started the car.

COMPANION

You press your ear to my ear
And we both hear the ocean.

WRITE WHAT YOU KNOW

Are you writing what you know,
When you mention the wind in the willows,
Or the glistening, midnight moon?

You very well may be.

Today I saw a vulture dragging a skunk carcass
Across a neighborhood road
Two feet away from a school zone.

And now, as I lay myself down for sleep,
I remember the other things from my day.
The things I know.

I remember the neck pain I woke with
And the bitterness of my morning cup.
I remember how the dogs avoided the grass
Due to the dew on their paws
I remember my love,
As she floated from corner to corner
Performing her daily dance,
How easily the day yields to her flourishes.

But just now,

As I am drifting off,
A flash of light,
A beam cutting through my mini-blinds,
I rise, make haste as you might say,
To draw the blinds,
To see something altogether new.

The wind is blowing the Sweet Gums
Gently below my window,
And each leaf is taking its turn
Reflecting into my room
The bright and glistening light
Of the midnight moon.

MAPLE TREE

The maple tree
In grandma's front yard
was chopped down this year.

BOOT

There is a small squeak
Coming from the old man's boot
As he limps along.

THE STATION AT MARIETTA

The station at Marietta was closed.
Not only closed but boarded.
Not only boarded, but overgrown.
With vines no longer verdant,
Dried against the stucco frame.
I find myself in vast country
In a small box with windows
Along the rivers,
Parallel to the interstate,
Behind the incorporated townships.
The pleasantries of travel—endless,
The Arbuckles breaking
Against the undulant Washita,
Wet, green pastures
With scattered, black cattle.
Fog, like blue talc
Descending into red dirt.
This ocean of color
Right outside the rails.
But the station at Marietta was closed.
Not only closed, but overgrown,
Not only overgrown, but colorless,
Like a once bustling tributary
Run dry.

HEATER

The house smells like dust
And tobacco from the pouch
When the heat comes on.

YOUR LIGHT

I imagine you in pressed linen,
Windblown, autumnal warmth,
Your freckles and my grins,
As I press into shade trees,
You press into light,
A setting sun, fading
Everywhere but your face,
As if you made it a home there,
Invited it in for a drink,
And it stayed.
I have no words when you are with me,
For what is there to say?
So I save them for solitude,
When you have brought your magic elsewhere
And I am still shaded by canopies
and memories of canopies,
Yet then comes a sliver,
Dancing and carving,
A golden beam cutting through magnolias
And memories of magnolias.
With my mind in full shade,
I lean my face into your light.

ABOUT THE AUTHOR

Mark Apel is the author *Dream Receipts, Peach Creek,* and *Parsonage* and lives in North Texas with his wife, daughter, and small dog.

If you enjoyed this book of poetry, please consider leaving a review wherever you review books.

Follow Mark Apel online at mdapel.com

Join Mark's mailing list at news.mdapel.com

Instagram – @mapelwrites

ALSO BY MARK APEL

Dream Receipts

Dream Receipts is a poetry travelogue of hallucinated journeys to Japan from author Mark Apel. *Dream Receipts* explores themes of escapism, depression, faith, shadows, daylight, night terrors, daydreaming, and the surreal beauty of an imagined Japan.

www.ingramcontent.com/pod-product-compliance
Lightning Source LLC
Chambersburg PA
CBHW020554030426
42337CB00013B/1099